TECHNOLOGY OF WAR

A STUNNING GUIDE TO THE HIGH-TECH WEAPONS AND VEHICLES OF MODERN WARFARE

Steve White

SCHOLASTIC
www.scholastic.com

Introduction

21ST-CENTURY WARFARE

The nature of war has changed dramatically. The **Cold War**, where America and its allies faced the Soviet Union (communist Russia and its supporters), ended with the collapse of the Soviet Union in 1989. However, the world remains an unsettled place.

New war zones have developed as local, territorial, and even tribal disputes that were once held in check were freed to suddenly flare up, requiring a rapid military response.

In addition, many of these new battle zones are in areas where it is hard to tell friend from foe, and where there is an ever-present risk of innocent civilians becoming casualties (known as collateral damage). This has meant that military interventions in the 21st century have had to become more precise as well as more rapid. Many of the weapons and vehicles used by America and its allies have been adapted to these new combat scenarios.

Robots and unmanned flying drones are part of the new technology of modern warfare.

2

GLOSSARY
Words that have been highlighted in **bold type** are explained on page 4

THE WAR

Following the
of 9/11, weap
unnecessary
conventional
uses in the W
targets were
While bridge
sometimes a
might be a m
preparing to
bomb. Anoth
terrorists oft
areas full of i

NEW TECHNOLOGY

To prevent innocent bystanders being harmed, gathering intelligence to ensure that the right targets were attacked became as vital as the weapons themselves. Meanwhile, these weapons were becoming much more accurate thanks to electronics and computers. While terrorists may fight with low-tech weapons, such as homemade bombs, the modern soldier can direct an unmanned drone on the other side of the world, via a satellite in space, to drop a self-guided bomb onto an enemy target.

This is the technology of war in the 21st century.

Essential Combat Gear

A soldier's uniform does a lot more than just identify him as a friend or an enemy. It also provides protection, camouflage, and storage for essential kit. A modern soldier in full uniform, with his helmet, body armor, equipment, and weapons, is carrying so much gear that he's said to be in full "battle rattle."

COMBAT UNFORM

U.S. combat uniforms are designed with well-positioned pockets, reinforcements, and padding, to help with carrying kit and supplies such as food, water, and ammunition.

Protective padding at the knees and elbows was suggested by soldiers with combat experience. Flame-resistant army combat uniforms (ACUs) are issued to protect against burns, especially in areas where improvised explosive devices (IEDs) are common.

Advanced combat helmet (ACH)
- Made from tough **synthetic** fibers, the ACH is armored but lightweight (the medium size weighs just 3.25 lb.).
- The ACH can resist **shrapnel**.
- Communication devices and night visio goggles can be added to the helmet.
- Padding and straps are designed to protect against blast injuries.

Camouflage:
- U.S. Army combat uniforms have the universal camouflage pattern (UCP) of tan, gray, and green.
- The uniforms of the U.S. Marines, Navy, and Air Force have camouflage patterns designed to suit their likely combat environments.

Meals on the move:
- On the battlefield, the main food eaten by U.S. Army troops is called the MRE (meal ready to eat).
- The entire meal is contained in a tough plastic pouch that is lightweight and easy to carry.

Army combat boots:
- Made from leather and nylon, these are both flame-resistant and water-resistant.
- They have special shock-absorbent soles and a tread pattern that gives grip in different terrains.

Improved outer tactical vest (IOTV):

- This armored vest protects a soldier from bullets and blast fragments.
- A medium-size IOTV can weigh up to 30 lb.
- The vest has four plate armor inserts (back, front, and sides) and extra plates can be added to protect the neck and groin.

M-16A4 rifle with M-203 grenade launcher:

- A soldier's personal weapons, such as this assault rifle, form part of his "battle rattle."

NIGHT VISION TECHNOLOGY

Infantry soldiers use high-tech devices that help them to see at night, or when visibility is poor.

AN/PAS-13 THERMAL WEAPON SIGHT (TWS):

This can be fitted to rifles or used separately. Instead of using light to produce an image, a TWS uses heat (warmer objects appear lighter). It can also be used to spot people or vehicles through fog or smoke.

AN/PVS-14 NIGHT VISION GOGGLE (NVG)

This is a helmet-mounted, flip-down, single-lens device that electronically boosts available light, such as moonlight, to give a clearer picture.

Personal Weapons

For the past two centuries, the soldier's main personal weapon has been the rifle, but rifle technology has advanced greatly in that time. There is also a range of other more specialized weapons that the modern infantryman can use.

THE M-4 CARBINE

The M-4 **carbine** is the standard-issue combat weapon for most U.S. infantry units and is also widely used by Special Forces around the world. It's a shorter, lighter version of the M-16A4 rifle and is better for close combat.

Although the M-16 is more accurate at a longer range, most infantry battles today take place at at much closer ranges (especially those in urban areas). This means that the M-4's advantages outweigh its disadvantages.

WEIGHT (WHEN LOADED): 7 lb.
LENGTH: stock extended: 33 in.; stock retracted: 29.7 in.
MAXIMUM RATE OF FIRE: 950 rounds per minute
MAXIMUM RANGE: 1,800 ft.
CALIBER: 5.56mm

An M-203 grenade launcher can be added.

The M-4 has two fire settings: semiautomatic (firing as fast as the user can pull the trigger) and automatic (the gun fires as long as the trigger is held back).

30-round magazine.

The Aimpoint M-68 close combat optic gunsight uses a red LED dot to show exactly where the bullet will hit the target.

The Picatinny rail adaptor system (RAS) is a bracket for attaching high-tech gunsights, flashlights, or night vision equipment.

A vertical forward grip can be added.

SQUAD SUPPORT WEAPONS

Specialized weapons and add-ons to personal weapons are used by individual soldiers to support their squad.

M-203A1 GRENADE LAUNCHER

- A pump-action, single-shot weapon that can be fitted under the barrel of personal weapons such as the M-16A4 and M-4.
- Is used with high explosives (HE) to deliver indirect fire on enemies hiding behind cover or in fortified positions.

AMMUNITION TYPE: high explosive, smoke grenades, tear gas, and antipersonnel rounds
MAXIMUM RANGE: 1,050 ft.
CALIBER: 40mm

M-136 AT-4 ANTITANK ROCKET LAUNCHER

- A single-use, lightweight antitank weapon, which enables infantry soldiers to disable or knock out armored vehicles and to destroy fortified positions, such as buildings.

WEIGHT: 14.8 lb.
AMMUNITION TYPE: high-explosive antitank projectiles
EFFECTIVE RANGE: 984 ft.
CALIBER: 84mm

M-249 LIGHT MACHINE GUN (SAW)

- There are usually two M-249 light machine guns (also known as squad automatic weapons or SAWs) issued to each eight-man U.S. Army squad.
- The M-249 has a folding bipod for steady firing when lying on the ground.
- It has a quick-change barrel that is easy to replace if it overheats from continuous firing.
- Ammunition is usually belt-fed into the M-249, but it can use M-4 and M-16 magazines in an emergency.

RATE OF FIRE: 775 rounds per minute
MAXIMUM RANGE: 10,200 ft.
CALIBER: 5.56mm

Countering the IED Threat

One of the greatest threats to the modern soldier is the IED—the improvised explosive device. Made from everyday materials, these homemade bombs can be just as effective as conventional bombs. New, high-tech gear has been developed to help counter these low-tech weapons.

ANATOMY OF AN IED

IEDs are inexpensive, but can inflict devastating damage. Over 60 percent of the casualties among coalition troops in Afghanistan are caused by IEDs. Their simplicity makes IEDs hard to detect, slowing down troop movements in areas where they are used.

IEDs have three parts:

- **Explosives.** These can be made from fertilizers, chemicals commonly found in kitchens, or propane gas.
- **A detonation system.** This triggers the explosives and is usually an electrical signal sent from a cell phone, a radio, or along a wire.
- **The casing.** This houses the explosives and disguises the device. It can be anything from a soda can to a car. Nails, ball bearings, screws, and metal rods are often included within the casing to make the explosion even more deadly.

THE BOMB SUIT

One of the most dangerous military jobs is that of an explosive ordnance disposal (EOD) specialist. Although robots are often used to deal with IEDs, a key piece of EOD kit is still the protective bomb suit.

A bomb suit usually has three layers:

- The outer layer is made of synthetic plate armor that actually hardens on the impact of shrapnel.
- Beneath this is a soft layer of specially made rubber or polyurethane. This absorbs the bomb's shock wave, which can be more dangerous than the shrapnel, as it causes damage to the lungs and brain.
- Finally, a layer of lightweight armor resists the last of the shrapnel.

The plates of the outer layer of armor are boomerang-shaped: the best shape to absorb the energy from a bomb blast.

Beneath the suit is a cooling layer that pumps ice water around the wearer's body—vital for EOD missions in hot countries, such as Afghanistan.

The helmet is equipped with a lamp, a cooling fan, a video camera, and radio.

The clear visor plate, called the strike face, is made of very tough multilayered synthetic material, which acts as a shock absorber.

The bomb suit comes with flame-resistant gloves, but many EOD technicians prefer to keep their hands bare as it is easier to handle complex tools.

EOD boots also include boomerang shaped blast plates.

BLAST PROTECTION

Vehicles—even tanks—can be damaged by IEDs or **mines**. To protect U.S. troops, mine-resistant vehicles have been developed.

THE MRAP

- MRAP stands for mine-resistant ambush-protected vehicle.

- It has a V-shaped underside, designed to deflect blasts and shrapnel away from the vehicle.

THE MMPV

- The medium mine-protected vehicle (MMPV) is used by EOD teams. It has a ramp at the back from which EOD robots (see pages 10–11) can be sent into action.

- The MMPV has a robotic arm that can be operated by a technician inside to deal with mines or IEDs.

Robots at War

Thanks to new technology, some of the dangerous jobs once done by military personnel are now being done by robots. These robots range from huge unmanned flying aircraft, through to robots the size of a toy.

THE TALON

The TALON is one of the main robots in use with the U.S. Army. It can be equipped for a number of different missions, from **reconnaissance** to actual combat, but its main job has been bomb disposal.

REMOTE CONTROL

Real robots aren't like those in the movies—they don't think and act for themselves. The TALON is controlled from an operator control unit (OCU) by a soldier using a hand controller. Signals are sent to the robot by radio or along a fiber-optic wire.

WEIGHT: 115 lb. (standard TALON)
LENGTH: 34 in.
WIDTH: 22.5 in.
MAXIMUM SPEED: (standard TALON) 5 mph
PAYLOAD: can carry 25 to 100 lb.
BATTERY LIFE: up to 4 hours

Antennae allow radio communication between the TALON robot and the OCU.

The TALON's robot arm is used to handle suspected bombs or IEDs for the explosive ordnance disposal (EOD) version. Other tools, such as special sensors to detect radiation, chemicals, gases, or fire, are fitted for the HAZMAT (hazardous materials) version.

TALON's powerful **caterpillar** tracks enable it to drive up stairs, through sand, and even on snow. It is also **amphibious** and can drive through water as well as on land.

Carries up to seven on-board cameras, which provide video to the operator. Night vision and heat-sensitive cameras help in poor visibility.

FRONT TOWARD ENEMY

Boston Dynamics

FUTURE ROBOTS

The U.S. Defense Advanced Research Projects Agency (DARPA) is developing futuristic military technology, including the DRC—the DARPA Robotic Challenge. These robots are intended to be part of a future U.S. military response to natural disasters, such as earthquakes or floods. As disaster areas are very dangerous, the robots would need to carry out rescue work on their own, using whatever equipment was available and even driving vehicles!

Digital Warfare

Advanced electronics and computers have had a huge impact on the technology of war. Computers, digital pictures, and video are vital tools for gathering military information and for communications. The Internet has also led to a whole new type of war—cyber war.

COMPUTERS AT WAR

Portable battlefield computers and digital devices are everywhere on modern battlefields. They are used for everything from instant communication to controlling robots. Handheld **global positioning system** (GPS) receivers use satellite signals to give soldiers their precise location, to send positions to commanders, and to make supporting fire more accurate. GPS technology is mounted in most military vehicles such as Humvees and tanks and helps to keep track of their movements. Thanks to computers and digital technology, intelligence can be instantly sent and received by soldiers engaged in combat.

An AN/PSC-5 Spitfire UHF manpack terminal can be used to make calls or to send reconnaissance images from a laptop by satellite.

CYBER WAR

One of the key battlefields today is the digital world of computers and the Internet. Every nation that uses computers is vulnerable to attack by **hackers**.

CYBERCOM

In May 2010, the U.S. Department of Defense created a new force: USCYBERCOM (United States Cyber Command). Its mission is to defend the U.S. against cyber attacks or to attack enemy computer networks.

MALWARE: CYBER ATTACK!

In most modern nations, the control of power, water, communication, and defense systems relies on computer technology. Terrorist computer hackers can launch cyber attacks by inserting malware (malicious software, such as viruses) into an enemy's computer systems. Malware can shut down power grids, disable defensive systems, disrupt communications, and create massive electrical blackouts.

HIGH-TECH SPIES

Advanced technology helps soldiers on the ground keep track of the enemy.

RECONNAISSANCE DRONES

Small, remote-controlled unmanned aerial vehicles (UAVs), such as the Dragon Eye, provide soldiers on the battlefield with advanced reconnaissance capabilities. The Dragon Eye sends live video of enemy positions and movements that can be viewed on a computer monitor.

The Dragon Eye is an unmanned aerial vehicle (UAV) that is guided by computers.

The Dragon Eye weighs just 5 lb. and comes as an easy-to-assemble kit that is small enough to be carried in a backpack.

On-board video cameras provide live footage of the ground below.

The video from the Dragon Eye is viewed on a computer monitor by soldiers on the ground.

SPIES IN SPACE

Reconnaissance satellites in orbit around the Earth, such as the U.S. Keyhole satellite, work like a giant digital camera in space. The Keyhole satellite takes black-and-white images of the Earth's surface so detailed that an object just 6 inches long, such as a book cover, can be read!

Main Battle Tank

The M-1 Abrams main battle tank (MBT) was originally designed to fight massive tank battles against invading Soviet forces during the Cold War. In the 21st century, it has successfully adapted to a new role, providing heavy firepower to support forces fighting the War on Terror.

Many recent conflicts have involved combat in urban areas, so the M-1 Abrams has been updated with a tank urban survival kit (TUSK). Improvements include extra armor fitted to its vulnerable rear, a protective shield and thermal sight for the loader's M-240 machine gun, and a remote-controlled system for the heavy machine gun, so that it can be fired while the crew is safely inside the tank.

The M-1's on-board fire control computer ensures 95 percent accuracy from its main gun.

M-1-A2 ABRAMS TANK

CREW: 4 (commander, driver, gunner, loader)
WEIGHT: 67.6 tons
LENGTH: 32.25 ft.
HEIGHT: 8 ft.
MAXIMUM SPEED: 42 mph
MAIN WEAPON: M-256 120mm **smoothbore** gun, effective range 2.5 mi.

The tank's high-tech plate armor, known as Chobham armor, is made from layers of steel, plastics, and ceramics and is highly impact resistant.

The gunner's primary sight has an optical sight for daylight viewing and a **thermal** imaging sight for nighttime. A laser rangefinder measures the exact distance to any target.

The M-1's turret has two six-tube M-250 grenade launchers. These fire smoke grenades to mask the tank's movements.

The front hull and turret of the M1-A2 has enhanced plate armor. This is made from super-dense depleted uranium, sandwiched between steel plates. Projectiles that hit these areas usually bounce off.

HIGH-TECH TANK AMMUNITION

The Abrams carries 42 rounds for its main M-256 smoothbore cannon. These include two main types of ammunition for use against armor or other hard targets:

• HEAT (high-explosive antitank) rounds. On impact these concentrate their explosive power on a very small area, so as to cut through enemy armor.
• Sabot rounds, such as the M-829A1, use ultra-high speed and high density to penetrate heavy armor. The M-829A1 is often called "the silver bullet" by tank crews.

HOW A SABOT ROUND WORKS

A sabot is a plastic case that fits around an antitank round with a long, narrow projectile inside (the penetrator). The sabot keeps the round centered in the gun barrel, which increases its speed (muzzle velocity).

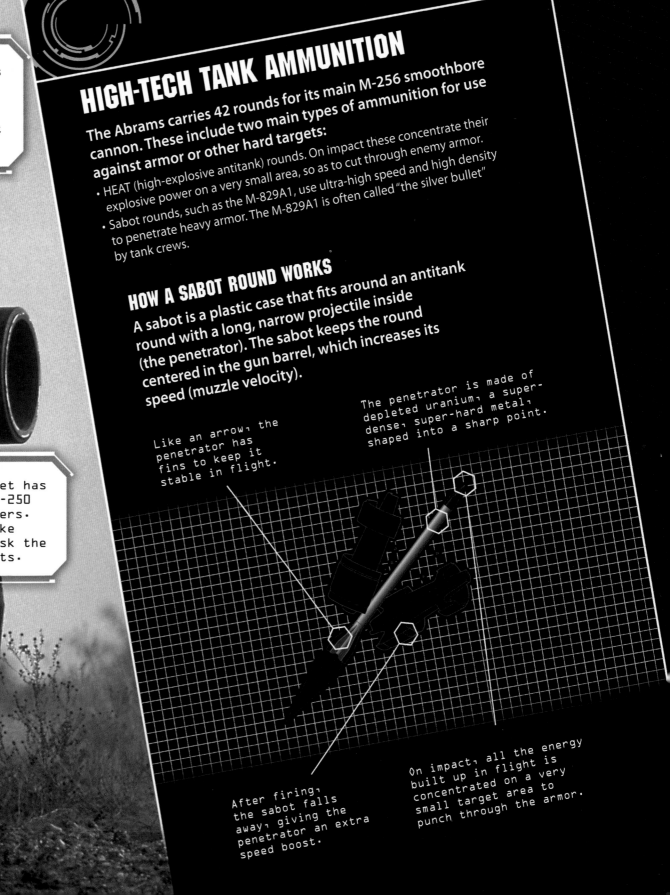

Like an arrow, the penetrator has fins to keep it stable in flight.

The penetrator is made of depleted uranium, a super-dense, super-hard metal, shaped into a sharp point.

After firing, the sabot falls away, giving the penetrator an extra speed boost.

On impact, all the energy built up in flight is concentrated on a very small target area to punch through the armor.

Battle Taxi

The Bradley armored vehicle may have had its origins in the Cold War, but it has played a key role in recent conflicts in Iraq and Afghanistan. It remains the U.S. Army's main "battle taxi" for transporting troops in war zones.

THE BRADLEY INFANTRY FIGHTING VEHICLE (IFV)

The Bradley is an armored personnel carrier (APC) that can carry a six-man infantry squad over rugged terrain or rough roads into battle. It's called an infantry fighting vehicle because troops can fight from the Bradley, or it can provide fire support while they dismount. Its main M-242 Bushmaster chain gun can destroy lightly armored vehicles, but the Bradley also carries antitank missiles.

THE BRADLEY M-2

WEIGHT: 27 tons
CREW: 3 (commander, gunner, driver)
COMBAT LOAD: 6 fully-equipped infantry soldiers
SPEED: 41 mph
ARMAMENT: 25mm M-242 chain gun, M-240 7.62mm machine gun, TOW antitank missiles

A launcher for two BGM-71 TOW (tube-launched, optically tracked, wire-guided) antitank missiles is mounted on the left of the turret.

Infantry soldiers deploy from a ramp at the rear. Two firing slits in the ramp enable troops inside to spot and fire at targets behind the Bradley, where it is most vulnerable.

THE M-242 BUSHMASTER CHAIN GUN

The Bradley's most devastating weapon is a single-barreled 25mm chain gun, fired by the gunner or commander.

- The M-242 can fire armor-piercing (AP) or high explosive (HE) rounds at a rate of up to 200 rounds per minute.
- Against enemy armor, it can also fire the M-919 APFSDS-T (armor-piercing, fin-stabilized, discarding sabot-tracer), which contains a dart of super-dense depleted uranium that can penetrate most armor on the modern battlefield.
- It's called a chain gun because it uses an electric-powered chain drive to feed and fire the weapon at high speed.

The main armament is a 25mm M-242 Bushmaster chain gun used against armor and hard targets. Mounted next to it is a 7.62mm M-240 machine gun.

THE M-3 CAVALRY FIGHTING VEHICLE

The M-3 cavalry fighting vehicle is very similar to the M-2, but its main role is scouting (gathering information and hunting for the enemy). It carries more ammunition and radios, but has a smaller, two-man scout team, sometimes equipped with their own handheld antitank missiles.

The body of the M-2 is made from aluminum and a laminate armor, formed from layers of different metals, ceramics, and plastics.

A layer of explosive-reactive armor (ERA) can be fitted to the turret and sides for extra protection. ERA tiles are designed to explode when struck by a shell or missile, canceling the explosive blast of the enemy weapon.

Four-Wheeled War Horse

The Humvee—or high-mobility multipurpose wheeled vehicle (HMMWV) as it is officially known—is a common sight wherever U.S. armed forces are sent. It is a lightweight, four-wheel drive vehicle that has many uses on the battlefield.

THE VERSATILE HUMVEE

The basic M-998 Humvee has been modified to handle a number of different missions on the modern battlefield. The U.S. military has eleven Humvee variants in service, including:

- M-1045 antitank versions equipped with a BGM-71 TOW antitank missile in a turret on the roof.
- M-997 ambulance versions that can carry up to four stretchers and eight walking wounded.
- M-1165 command and control versions, fitted with long-range communications electronics for radio operators and a battlefield commander.
- Expanded capacity vehicle (ECV) variants that can carry more troops and heavier payloads.

The cab seats four, including the driver.

Many Humvees have self-recovery winches that can be used to pull the vehicle out if it gets stuck.

THE M-998 HUMVEE

WEIGHT: 5,200–5,900 lb.
LENGTH: 11 ft.
WIDTH: 7 ft.
TOP SPEED: 70 mph
WEAPONS: The Humvee can carry:
- Mark-19 grenade machine gun
- M-2 .50-caliber machine gun
- M-134 mini-gun
- M-240 machine gun
- TOW antitank missile launcher
- Stinger surface-to-air-missiles

Being low, wide, and long makes the Humvee very stable and resistant to rolling over on uneven roads and rough terrain.

The chassis is made from steel bars and aluminum body panels. These are designed to bend and act as shock absorbers.

LASER FIREPOWER

One of the more high-tech Humvees is equipped with a powerful laser, which is used to destroy unexploded bombs and IEDs. The laser system is called ZEUS-HLONS (HMMWV Laser Ordnance Neutralization System) and has been used in Iraq and Afghanistan—the first time a laser has been fired on a battlefield.

HOW A LASER HUMVEE WORKS

The long-range laser beam means that the Humvee can remain at a safe distance, up to 820 feet from its target.

A joystick control aims the laser very accurately at IEDs or exposed mines.

Unexploded mines

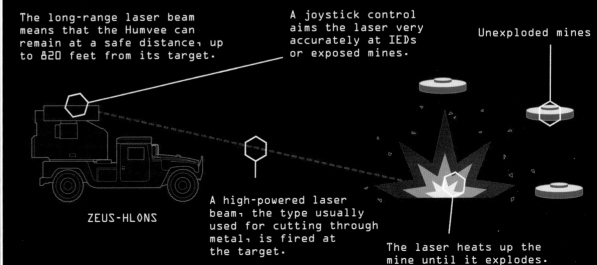

ZEUS-HLONS

A high-powered laser beam, the type usually used for cutting through metal, is fired at the target.

The laser heats up the mine until it explodes.

High-Tech Bombers

Bombers are still one of the United States Air Force's (U.S.A.F.) most powerful longe-range weapons. They can deliver heavy bomb loads over great distances and a few bombers can drop as many bombs as squadrons of smaller jets, with equal accuracy. The U.S.A.F. has three types of bomber in service.

The trailing edge uses a double-W shape.

THE B-2: STEALTH TECHNOLOGY

The easiest way to detect a flying aircraft is with radar (short for radio detecting and ranging). Radar fires radio waves into the air and collects any waves that bounce back. These signals can reveal the distance and direction of a target.

Stealth aircraft, such as the B-2, have a shape that is designed to scatter radar signals rather than bounce them back. They are also built with materials that absorb radar waves. These features make the B-2 Spirit stealth bomber almost invisible to radar.

The B-2 can carry both conventional and nuclear weapons, including up to 80 500 lb. joint direct attack munition bombs (JDAMs); 30,000 lb. massive ordnance penetrator bombs (MOPs); B-61 and B-63 nuclear bombs; or AGM-129 advanced cruise missiles.

The B-2 has a crew of two. The pilot sits on the left and the mission commander on the right.

B-2 SPIRIT

CREW: 2
WINGSPAN: 172 ft.
LENGTH: 69 ft.
WEIGHT: 160,000 lb.
BOMB LOAD: 40,000 lb.
MAX. ALTITUDE: 50,000 ft.
SPEED: 630 mph
RANGE: 6,900 mi.
NUMBER IN SERVICE: 20

B-52H STRATOFORTRESS

CREW: 5
WINGSPAN: 185 ft.
LENGTH: 159 ft.
WEIGHT: 185,000 lb.
BOMB LOAD: 70,000 lb.
MAX. ALTITUDE: 50,000 ft.
SPEED: 630 mph
RANGE: 10,059 mi.
NUMBER IN SERVICE: 85 (plus 9 in reserve)

- Can deliver both nuclear and conventional weapons.
- Capable of dropping the widest range of weapons of any aircraft in the U.S.A.F.
- Can carry up to 20 conventional cruise missiles.

B-1B LANCER

CREW: 4
MAX. WINGSPAN: 137 ft.
LENGTH: 146 ft.
WEIGHT: 192,000 lb.
BOMB LOAD: 75,000 lb.
MAX. ALTITUDE: 30,000 ft.
MAX. SPEED: 828 mph
RANGE: 7,495 mi.
NUMBER IN SERVICE: 66

- Nicknamed the "bone" (B-one).
- Has movable "swing" wings. The forward settings are for takeoff and landing, midair refueling, and some high-altitude weapon releases. The swept-back settings are for high-speed flights.
- Carries the largest bomb load of any aircraft in the U.S.A.F.

The leading edge of the wing is set at an angle of 33°.

The body of the aircraft is made from advanced **composite** materials that are stronger and lighter than steel.

The B-2's curved shape deflects radar beams. It is also covered with a new radar-absorbent material (RAM) called alternate high-frequency material (AHFM). Four robots spray this onto the B-2 while it is being built.

Super-Fighter

Control of the skies over a battlefield is the key mission of modern fighter airplanes. Although close-range aerial combat is rare today, stealth technology and long-range homing missiles help to achieve air supremacy.

THE F-22 RAPTOR

The F-22 Raptor is primarily designed for air-to-air engagements, but it can also support missions on the ground. Like the B-2 stealth bomber, the Raptor's shape helps it to avoid detection both visually and by radar. The sloped edges of its surfaces scatter radar waves and it is also painted with radar-absorbent materials (RAM). This technology makes it very difficult for the enemy to locate the F-22 Raptor.

The Raptor is highly maneuverable at any speed and capable of very tight turns.

The pilot can detect approaching aircraft from up to 150 miles away using the Raptor's AN/APG-77 radar system.

The Raptor has a six-bareled M61A2 20mm Vulcan cannon in its right wing, with 480 rounds of ammunition.

For increased stealth, three weapons bays with missiles or bombs are housed within the body of the aircraft.

CREW: 1
WEIGHT (FULLY LOADED): 49,540 lb.
LENGTH: 62.1 ft.
WINGSPAN: 44.6 ft.
TOP SPEED: 1,500 mph
RANGE: 1,840 mi.
NUMBER IN SERVICE: 195

The exhaust nozzles of the two engines can be moved up or down (known as thrust vectoring) to increase maneuverability.

GLASS COCKPIT

Modern fighter aircraft, such as the F-22, have "glass cockpits." All of the traditional flying instruments have been replaced by four main computer screens and a heads-up display (HUD) on which vital flight, targeting, and radar information is displayed. Computers run many of the aircraft's flight systems, freeing up the pilot to concentrate on the combat mission.

HANDS-ON CONTROLS

The pilot of the F-22 Raptor uses specially developed controls called HOTAS (hands-on throttle and stick). All the vital controls are on the throttle (which controls the power of the engines) and the joystick (which steers the aircraft). In a combat situation, the pilot can select weapons and targets, adjust his radar screen, change channels on his radio, and perform many other functions by simply moving a finger or thumb.

HIGH-TECH HELMET

The pilot of the Lockheed Martin F-35 Lightning II uses an even more futuristic helmet-mounted display system (HMDS). Many of the fighter's control panels are projected onto the visor of his helmet, which is also equipped with day and night vision cameras and video from the fighter's detection systems.

The F-22 can carry up to six medium-range air-to-air missiles in its central weapons bay, plus one short-range air-to-air missile in the smaller bays either side.

Fire and Forget: Guided Missiles

Air-to-air missiles (AAMs) with built-in guidance systems can steer themselves to an enemy aircraft after they have been fired. These "smart" weapons are also known as "fire and forget" missiles, because a pilot can launch one and leave it to destroy the target while he flies clear.

AIM-9 SIDEWINDER

The AIM-9 (air intercept missile) Sidewinder is a short-range, self-guiding missile designed to destroy enemy aircraft in air-to-air combat. It uses heat sensors to steer itself toward the **infrared** heat energy of an enemy airplane's jet engine exhaust. Older versions had to be fired from behind the enemy aircraft to lock onto its engines. Newer versions, such as the AIM-9X, have super-cooled seeker heads that can sense heat from any part of the target and can be fired from any direction.

GUIDANCE: infrared heat-seeking missile
WEIGHT: 188 lb.
LENGTH: 9 ft. 5 in.
TOP SPEED: 1,903 mph (**Mach** 2.5—that's 2.5 times the speed of sound!)
RANGE: 18 mi.

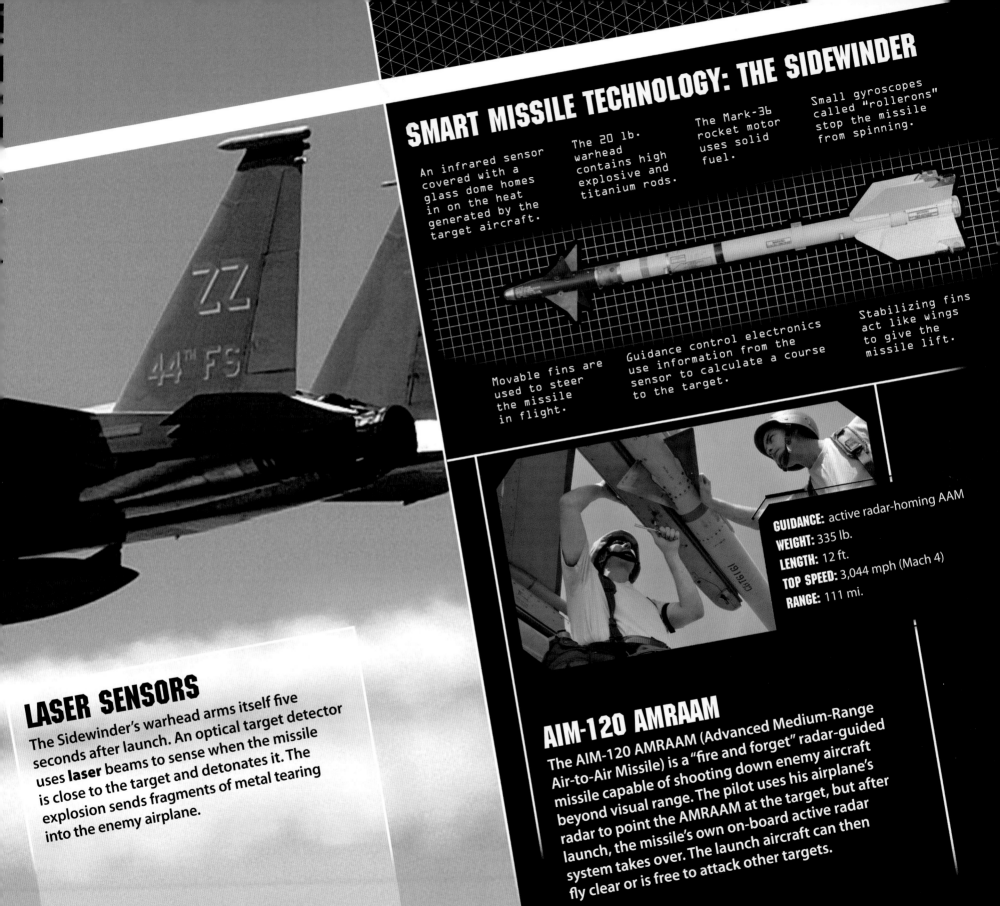

SMART MISSILE TECHNOLOGY: THE SIDEWINDER

An infrared sensor covered with a glass dome homes in on the heat generated by the target aircraft.

The 20 lb. warhead contains high explosive and titanium rods.

The Mark-36 rocket motor uses solid fuel.

Small gyroscopes called "rollerons" stop the missile from spinning.

Movable fins are used to steer the missile in flight.

Guidance control electronics use information from the sensor to calculate a course to the target.

Stabilizing fins act like wings to give the missile lift.

GUIDANCE: active radar-homing AAM
WEIGHT: 335 lb.
LENGTH: 12 ft.
TOP SPEED: 3,044 mph (Mach 4)
RANGE: 111 mi.

AIM-120 AMRAAM

The AIM-120 AMRAAM (Advanced Medium-Range Air-to-Air Missile) is a "fire and forget" radar-guided missile capable of shooting down enemy aircraft beyond visual range. The pilot uses his airplane's radar to point the AMRAAM at the target, but after launch, the missile's own on-board active radar system takes over. The launch aircraft can then fly clear or is free to attack other targets.

LASER SENSORS

The Sidewinder's warhead arms itself five seconds after launch. An optical target detector uses **laser** beams to sense when the missile is close to the target and detonates it. The explosion sends fragments of metal tearing into the enemy airplane.

Smart Bombs

Accuracy is vital for modern bombing missions. The target can often be a terrorist group in a house surrounded by the homes of innocent families. "Smart" bombs enable pilots to destroy targets without harming people or buildings close by (known as "collateral damage").

PRECISION TARGETING

A smart bomb has an on-board guidance system that enables it to hit a target with great accuracy. Laser guidance, GPS satellite signals, or a mix of the two, steer the bomb to a target after it has been dropped.

LASER-GUIDED BOMBS

Laser-guided bombs (LGBs) lock onto a laser beam shone onto a target by an airplane or by troops on the ground using a laser target designator. Modern LGBs can hit targets to within 27 feet of the aim point, at a range of over nine miles.

PAVEWAY

Paveway is the name for a laser guidance system that can be added to normal bombs to make them into laser-guided bombs (LGBs).

- The Paveway kit includes a laser seeker on the nose and moving fins on the tail, which guide the bomb to its target.
- Bad weather, smoke, and fog can interfere with the laser system, so an enhanced version of Paveway uses GPS satellite guidance as a backup.

LENGTH: 14ft. 5in.
WARHEAD: 500 to 2,000 lb.
RANGE: 9 mi.

The laser beam reflects off the target, creating a target zone (called the basket) that the bomb can lock onto.

A laser beam is directed at the target. This is called "painting" the target.

A soldier shines a laser target designator onto a target.

JOINT DIRECT ATTACK MUNITION

Joint direct attack munition (JDAM) is a kit that can be added to standard bombs to make them into smart, satellite-guided weapons. It includes a GPS guidance system and tail fins that steer the bomb as it falls.

- A JDAM can land within 32 feet of its target.
- The position of the target is loaded onto the JDAM's on-board GPS guidance system.
- A GPS is not affected by smoke, cloud, or fog, so unlike laser-guided bombs, JDAMs can be used in bad weather.

LENGTH: up to 12.75 ft.
WARHEAD: 1,000 to 2,000 lb.
RANGE: 17 mi.

WEIGHT: 285 lb.
WARHEAD: 206 lb.
RANGE: 60 mi.

The bomb is dropped into the basket and uses its fins to steer itself to the target.

The LGB is a "smart" weapon and can steer itself, but the target needs to be continuously "painted" by the laser until the bomb has hit.

SMALL-DIAMETER BOMB

The small-diameter bomb (SDB) is a precision satellite-guided weapon, accurate to within 24 feet of the aim point. This accuracy, together with its small warhead size, greatly reduces the chance of collateral damage.

- The SDB uses GPS to guide itself to its target (this is known as "brilliant" technology, as it doesn't need any help from the launch aircraft).
- "Diamondback" wings open on release, so the SDB can glide to its target.
- The SDB is capable of punching through three feet of reinforced concrete.

Cruise Missiles

Attacking heavily defended targets in an airplane is very risky, so many bombing missions are now undertaken by cruise missiles. These are small, unmanned, flying bombs that can hit targets with great accuracy from hundreds of miles away.

After a rocket-powered launch, the Tomahawk switches to a **turbofan** jet engine to fly. This gives off little heat, making it hard for infrared heat sensors to detect.

THE TOMAHAWK

The Tomahawk is a long-range, self-guided missile, usually launched from ships or submarines. It flies at high speed, close to the ground to avoid detection by enemy radar. This cruise missile can carry a variety of warheads, from 1,000 pounds of high explosive to a devastating nuclear warhead.

LENGTH: 18.3 ft.
WINGSPAN: 8.9 ft.
SPEED: 550 mph
RANGE: varies according to version. The missile with the maximum range is the BGM-109A Tomahawk land attack cruise missile, which carries a W-80 nuclear warhead and can hit targets up to 1,550 miles away.

Movable tail fins steer the Tomahawk in flight.

AIR-LAUNCHED CRUISE MISSILES

While most cruise missiles are designed to be launched from ships or submarines, there are also air-launched versions, carried by the U.S.A.F.'s B-52H Stratofortress bombers.

AGM-86 ALCM

The AGM-86 is an air-launched cruise missile (ALCM), carried by the B-52H bomber (see page 21). It can be armed with a nuclear warhead or a standard explosive warhead. It travels at speeds of up to 550 mph and has a range of more than 1,500 miles.

Pop-out wings are folded against the body until after launch, when they open out to steady the missile's flight.

83

Guidance section, containing the GPS system and sensors.

AGM-129 ADVANCED CRUISE MISSILE

This advanced version of the cruise missile uses stealth technology. It has an irregular shape and forward-pointing wings that make it harder to detect by enemy radar. It is also carried and launched by the B-52H bomber.

TARGET-FINDING TECHNOLOGY

Cruise missiles such as the Tomahawk use several types of guidance system to find their targets. These allow the missile to fly low at low altitude, following roads, dodging defenses, and steering around obstacles such as hills.

RADAR

The RGM/UGM-109B Tomahawk antiship missile uses an on-board radar guidance system. It skims the sea at wave-top height to destroy enemy ships.

GPS

Cruise missiles use signals from GPS satellites to pinpoint their own position and to find their way to a target.

TERCOM
(terrain contour matching)

During flight, the missile uses its radar to compare the hills and valleys below to a digital map loaded onto its on-board computer before launch. TERCOM lets the missile fly close to the ground.

DSMAC
(digital scene mapping area correlation)

The missile finds its target by scanning the ground and comparing what it "sees" with a digital image loaded before launch.

Unmanned Aircraft: Flying Drones

Many missions that were once flown by piloted aircraft are now being flown by UAVs—unmanned aerial vehicles. Also known as drones or RPAs (remotely piloted aircraft), they can be flown by pilots in control centers a continent away.

Power comes from a Rotax 914 engine (the same type of engine used on many snowmobiles).

Two-bladed "pusher" propeller.

THE PREDATOR DRONE

Drones supply real-time reconnaissance images without putting pilots at risk. They range from small, hand-launched airplanes to huge RPAs such as the Predator. The Predator is controlled from a ground control station (GCS) which communicates with the drone via satellite. A pilot flies the Predator by remote control, while a sensor operator studies the images sent back from its cameras.

WEIGHT (FULLY LOADED): 2,250 lb.
LENGTH: 27 ft.
WINGSPAN: 66 ft.
TOP SPEED: 135 mph
RANGE: 675 mi.

The Predator has "wet wings," which have tiny holes on the front edge that "weep" glycol—an antifreeze that stops the wings icing over.

The Predator comes in two models: the RQ-1 reconnaissance version and the MQ-1, which is armed with two AGM-115 Hellfire missiles. These can be used to attack targets or to provide fire support to troops.

THE MQ-9 REAPER

A larger and more powerful version of the Predator, the MQ-9 Reaper is specifically designed for attack missions.

- It has a more powerful engine than the Predator, so it can carry a weapons load fifteen times greater than the MQ-1.

- The Reaper is fitted with a laser rangefinder/designator that "paints" targets for its laser-guided weapons, such as the AGM-114 Hellfire missile or Paveway LGBs.

- It can fly for up to fourteen hours while fully loaded.

The Predator's nose houses a color camera, a daylight TV camera, and a heat-sensitive infrared camera for use at night.

The Predator has a laser rangefinder/ designator ball housed in a bubble on the nose. This gives accurate distances to targets, and can be used to "paint" targets to direct laser-guided bombs and missiles.

ROBOT AIRPLANES: THE BOEING X-45

The X-45 Phantom represents the next generation of UAVs. It is a completely robotic aircraft that can fly itself and which can make its own decisions during a mission.

- The X-45 is designed for stealth, to slip into heavily defended airspace and knock out enemy defenses.

- It has "artificial intelligence" built into an on-board computer, which allows the X-45 to maneuver and attack without any input from controllers on the ground.

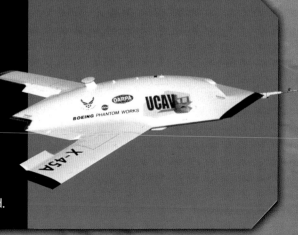

Surface-to-Air Missiles

Surface-to-air missiles (SAMs) are a powerful defensive weapon used in modern conflicts. They have a longer range than any gun and can shoot down incoming enemy missiles.

THE MIM-104 PATRIOT

Patriot missiles are the main antiair defense system used by U.S. forces. These SAMs are designed to destroy both enemy aircraft and missiles. There are two main types of Patriot in service with U.S. forces.

PAC-2 GEM+ (GUIDANCE ENHANCED MISSILE PLUS)

This updated version of the original Patriot has improved radar, capable of detecting smaller targets, which makes it particularly effective against missiles. It uses a "proximity" fuse, which makes the Patriot explode near its target rather than hit it. The target is destroyed by pieces of the missile's warhead.

PAC-3

This version of the Patriot has advanced radar and computer guidance systems for "hit to kill" attacks on enemy airplanes and missiles. Rather than use a proximity fuse, the PAC-3 actually hits its target. It has small rocket engines to make in-flight corrections to its course, greatly increasing the missile's accuracy.

PATRIOT PAC-2
LENGTH: 17.4 ft.
WEIGHT: 2,000 lb.

PATRIOT PAC-3
LENGTH: 17.1 ft.
WEIGHT: 688 lb.
RANGE: 43 mi.
SPEED: 3,800 mph+

PAC-2 Patriots have a 200 pound fragmentation warhead. Four PAC-2s are carried by the M-901 launcher.

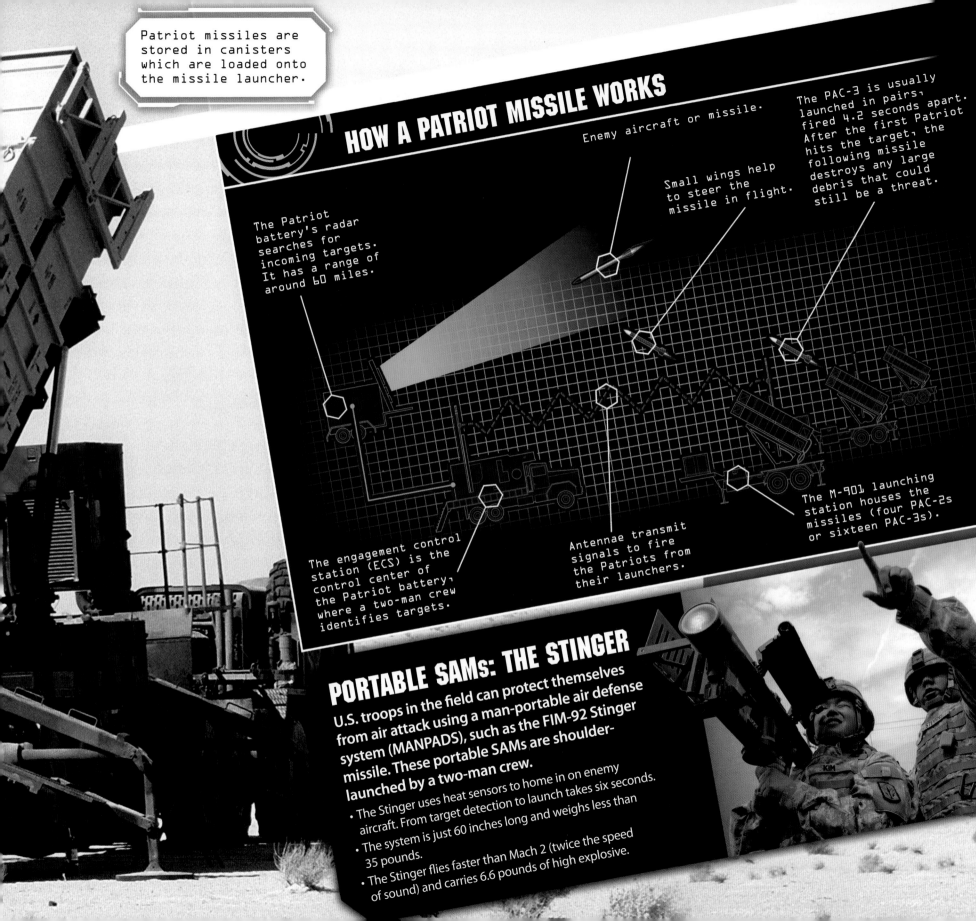

Patriot missiles are stored in canisters which are loaded onto the missile launcher.

HOW A PATRIOT MISSILE WORKS

The Patriot battery's radar searches for incoming targets. It has a range of around 60 miles.

Enemy aircraft or missile.

Small wings help to steer the missile in flight.

The PAC-3 is usually launched in pairs, fired 4.2 seconds apart. After the first Patriot hits the target, the following missile destroys any large debris that could still be a threat.

The engagement control station (ECS) is the control center of the Patriot battery, where a two-man crew identifies targets.

Antennae transmit signals to fire the Patriots from their launchers.

The M-901 launching station houses the missiles (four PAC-2s or sixteen PAC-3s).

PORTABLE SAMs: THE STINGER

U.S. troops in the field can protect themselves from air attack using a man-portable air defense system (MANPADS), such as the FIM-92 Stinger missile. These portable SAMs are shoulder-launched by a two-man crew.

- The Stinger uses heat sensors to home in on enemy aircraft. From target detection to launch takes six seconds.
- The system is just 60 inches long and weighs less than 35 pounds.
- The Stinger flies faster than Mach 2 (twice the speed of sound) and carries 6.6 pounds of high explosive.

Steel Rain: the MLRS

The standard MLRS rocket contains submunitions—small, high-explosive "bomblets" that rain down upon the enemy.

The MLRS uses "shoot and scoot" tactics, firing its rockets and moving to a new firing position. This makes it difficult for enemy fire to lock onto the MLRS.

The M-270 MLRS (multiple launch rocket system) is the latest in self-propelled artillery on the modern battlefield. It can unleash a shower of high explosive upon a target, which has earned MLRS strikes the nickname "steel rain."

THE M-270 MLRS

The M-270 is a mobile fire support vehicle with an M-269 launcher loader module (LLM) mounted on an M-993 carrier vehicle. The LLM carries two pods, holding either six rockets or one MGM-140 army tactical missile. The LLM's rockets or missiles can be fired in less than one minute at targets up to 28 miles away.

The M-270's caterpillar tracks make it capable of driving over rough ground, sand, or snow.

A twelve-rocket MLRS strike can drop a "steel rain" of 8,000 high-explosive submunitions over an area of almost one-third of a square mile.

ARMY TACTICAL MISSILE SYSTEM (ATACMS)

The ATACMS missile is a longer-range weapon that can be fired by the MLRS. It is designed to destroy larger, more heavily defended enemy targets at ranges of up to nearly 200 miles. An ATACMS missile can carry various quantities of M-74 antitank or antipersonnel **submunitions** or a 500 pound explosive warhead.

MLRS ROCKETS

The MLRS fires various kinds of rockets. The basic rocket—the M-26, has a range of 20 miles and carries 644 M-77 dual-purpose improved conventional munitions (DPICM) which can be used against enemy soldiers or armored vehicles. Other versions have extended ranges, different warheads, or are fitted with GPS for improved accuracy.

CREW: 3 (commander, gunner, section chief)
WEIGHT: 27.5 tons
LENGTH: 22.6 ft.
WIDTH: 9.9 ft.
TOP SPEED: 40 mph

Rockets can be fired singly or in batches from two to twelve rockets. Between each rocket firing, the MLRS's fire control computer re-aims the LLM to make sure each rocket stays on target.

HIMARS: THE MINI-MLRS

The M-142 HIMARS (high-mobility artillery rocket system) is a 5-ton truck modified to carry just one LLM pod, carrying either six rockets or one missile. Being lighter and smaller it is faster, with a top speed of up to 53 mph. The M-142 uses the same fire control systems used on the most up-to-date version of the MLRS, and takes just sixteen seconds to aim and fire its rockets.

Apache Attack Helicopter

The AH-64D Apache is one of the U.S. Army's most technologically advanced combat helicopters. Armed with a range of high-tech weaponry, the Apache can make devastating attacks on enemy ground forces, includinag tanks.

THE AH-64D LONGBOW APACHE

The Apache Longbow is a heavily armored attack helicopter with a powerful range of armaments for ground support missions. The Longbow version of the Apache is equipped with advanced sensor and fire control technology. With these systems the Longbow Apache is highly effective at spotting, tracking, and destroying targets on the ground.

CREW: 2 (pilot, copilot/gunner)
ROTOR DIAMETER: 48 ft.
BODY LENGTH: 49.5 ft.
SPEED: 165 mph
RANGE: 300 mi.

Black Hole infrared and heat suppression system. Nozzles feed the cool air flowing around the Apache into the hot engine exhaust gases, cooling them and making it harder for enemy heat-seeking missiles to track the helicopter.

Each wing has two weapon pylons with four launch rails for AGM-115 Hellfire antitank missiles. These are usually laser-guided by the Apache's fire control systems, but more advanced versions use built-in radar to hit their targets.

The Apache can also carry Hydra-70 rocket launcher pods which fire nineteen 2.75 in. FFARs (folding fin aerial rockets). FFARs can be fitted with various warheads, including high explosive and antipersonnel versions that spray lethal metal darts at enemy troops.

Four-bladed main rotor. The front edge of each blade is made of strong titanium metal. It can withstand the impact of branches or aerials when the Apache is flying low.

The two aircrew sit one in front of the other, with the pilot behind the gunner. The cockpit is heavily armored and both positions have flight controls, so that the copilot can maneuver the helicopter if the pilot is hit.

An M-230 30mm chain gun is the primary weapon for ground support missions, such as strafing enemy troops, fortified positions, or lightly armored vehicles. It is fed by a magazine containing up to 1,200 high-explosive rounds and can fire 650 rounds per minute.

HIGH-TECH SENSORS

FIRE CONTROL RADAR

The Apache's AN/APG-78 Longbow fire control radar (FCR) uses radio waves to spot and identify targets. It can track up to 128 targets at the same time, and can select the sixteen most dangerous targets and direct weapons at them within 30 seconds.

TARGETING TECH

A rotating turret houses a target acquisition and designation system (TADS) as well as a pilot night vision system (PNVS) for use in poor visibility. The turret is equipped with a TV camera, a heat-sensitive camera, and a laser designator/rangefinder that paints targets for laser-guided weapons.

HELMET-MOUNTED SIGHT

One of the most advanced features of the Apache's fire control system is the integrated helmet and display sighting system (IHADSS). A special lens mounted on a flight helmet aims the Apache's M-230 chain gun. The IHADSS system tracks the movement of the pilot's head and eyes and sends this information to the gun, so that where the pilot looks, the gun aims!

Transformers: the Tilt-rotor

The tilt-rotor is a new type of aircraft that has a key military transport role. It can take off without a runway, like a helicopter, but then transforms into a speedy turboprop airplane. This has made it invaluable for transporting troops and cargo for military operations.

THE V-22 OSPREY

The V-22 Osprey is a vertical takeoff and landing (VTOL) aircraft that can launch, hover, and land like a helicopter, but can also fly long distances at high speed like an airplane. It does this by rotating its engine pods.

A VTOL aircraft, such as the Osprey, has a number of military advantages. Like a helicopter, it can take off and land in small areas where it's impossible to use a transport airplane. In airplane mode, it can fly faster and farther than a helicopter and can carry greater loads.

CREW: 4 (pilot, copilot, two flight engineers)
BODY LENGTH: 57 ft.
WINGSPAN: 45 ft.
WEIGHT: 47,500 lb.
MAXIMUM SPEED: 315 mph
RANGE: up to 580 mi.
LOAD: 24 troops seated or 32 standing; internal cargo 20,000 lb.

Cockpit for the pilot and copilot. There is a foldout seat for a flight engineer.

The cargo bay is 21 feet long and 6 feet wide. There are foldout seats for 24 troops. The Osprey can carry 20,000 pounds of cargo inside the bay or 15,000 pounds outside, slung beneath the aircraft on cargo hooks and cables.

Each propeller has three blades that are 38 feet long. Both the blades and the wings can be folded for compact storage aboard an aircraft carrier.

The Osprey is powered by two Rolls Royce/Allison AE 1107C turboshaft engines, which each drive a giant propeller to provide both lift and forward thrust.

Rear ramp for loading and unloading vehicles, cargo, or troops. The Osprey can be armed with M-2 .50-caliber or M-240 machine guns mounted on the ramp to provide fire support for infantry in a combat assault landing.

HOW A TILT-ROTOR WORKS

1. For takeoff or landing, the engine pods are in an upright position. The propellers act like the rotors on a twin-engined helicopter to create vertical lift.

2. Once the tilt-rotor is in the air, the transition from vertical to horizontal flight can be made. Power from the engines is tapped to rotate the engine pods into a forward position.

3. In just twelve seconds the rotor blades are facing forward like the propellers on an airplane. The wings now create the lift to keep the tilt-rotor in the air, which flies like a regular propeller-driven airplane.

Supercarrier

An aircraft carrier is basically a floating airbase. These ships are some of the biggest afloat, carrying a range of aircraft to provide vital air support in conflict zones. The latest aircraft carriers, soon to enter service with the U.S. Navy, are the Gerald R. Ford-class supercarriers.

THE FORD-CLASS SUPERCARRIER

Designed and built using computers and virtual reality blueprints, Ford-class aircraft carriers will utilize advanced technology throughout. Each of these colossal supercarriers is powered by two nuclear reactors, which supply electricity to drive the engines and the ship's other systems, including a new electromagnetic aircraft launch system.

Advanced robotic systems keep the crew to a minimum on Ford-class carriers. Fully automated systems move weapons to be mounted on aircraft from storage areas (magazines) to loading bays below the flight deck. Fully armed aircraft are then lifted up to the flight deck by elevators, ready for launch.

The "island" is the command center of the ship where the captain and his staff control operations aboard the carrier. Ford-class carriers have a much smaller island positioned farther back than on earlier carriers. Its location and shape make it difficult for enemy radar to locate.

Ford-class carriers are designed to carry around 90 aircraft of various types, including:

F/A-18E/F Super Hornet combat aircraft and a special version, the EA-18G Growler, used to attack enemy radar and antiaircraft defenses. These will soon be joined by the F-35 Lightning II joint strike fighter (see also pp. 22-23).

E2C/D Hawkeye AWACS (airborne warning and control system) aircraft. These provide an airborne radar station and extend the ship's ability to detect distant targets or threats.

SH-60/MH-60S Seahawk helicopters, used for search and rescue missions and to hunt enemy submarines, which are the greatest threat to aircraft carriers.

ELECTROMAGNETIC LAUNCH SYSTEM

Ford-class carriers have four catapults to help to launch aircraft from the short runways on the flight deck. A new electromagnetic aircraft launch system (EMALS) will be used, which uses electromagnetic waves to drive a metal carriage at high speed along a rail 330 feet long. This carriage can tow a 100,000 pound aircraft along, rapidly speeding it up to 149 mph to catapult it off the ship.

A metal carriage is propelled along the rail by electromagnetic waves created by the carrier's nuclear power plant.

Aircraft are attached to the carriage by detachable cables.

A fixed metal rail runs along a groove under the flight deck.

SUPERCARRIER WEAPONS

Aircraft carriers are large targets for enemy missiles fired from aircraft or from weapons on land. To counter this threat, Ford-class carriers are armed with a variety of self-defense weapons.

MISSILES

- RIM-162 Evolved Sea Sparrow Missile (ESSM) is a surface-to-air missile, designed to shoot down aircraft and missiles at a range of up to 27 miles.

- RIM-116 rolling airframe missile (RAM) is a launching system that holds eleven surface-to-air missiles per launcher and can destroy targets at a range of 5.6 miles.

LAST-DITCH DEFENSES: CIWS

The carrier's last line of defense against attack is the Phalanx CIWS (close-in weapon system). This is a radar-guided Vulcan 20mm cannon on a swiveling mount, which automatically tracks and shoots down antiship missiles or enemy aircraft if they slip through the ship's other defenses.

Nuclear Submarines

The stealth and massive firepower of submarines make them a key weapon for the U.S. Navy. Attack submarines (SSNs) are designed to destroy enemy ships and carry out reconnaissance missions, while ballistic missile submarines (SSBNs) provide a seagoing platform for launching nuclear missiles.

Dive planes: these act like small wings, helping the sub to move up or down while submerged.

The Ohio is powered by a S8G PWR nuclear reactor, which provides unlimited cruising time without the need to refuel.

A four-bladed propeller drives the submarine through the water.

OHIO-CLASS SUBMARINES

The U.S. Navy's Ohio-class submarines are among the most advanced submarines ever built. The U.S. Navy has two types in service. SSBNs (called "boomers") carry long-range nuclear missiles, such as the Trident II SLBM (submarine-launched ballistic missile). **SSGN**s carry conventional armaments, such as Tomahawk cruise missiles with high-explosive warheads. Both types launch their missiles while submerged. Ohio-class SSGNs can also launch flying drones to carry out reconnaissance missions.

Ohio-class submarines usually patrol at sea for 70 to 90 days at a time. Each sub has two completely separate crews, called Blue and Gold. While one crew is at sea, the other is resting and training ashore.

Each Ohio SSBN has 24 missile launch tubes built in. These are arranged in two rows with hatches on top of the deck and contain Trident missiles. In SSGN versions, 22 of the missile tubes have been replaced with multiple all-up round canisters (MACs), each loaded with a Tomahawk cruise missile. The remaining two tubes are fitted with an Advanced SEAL Delivery System (ASDS). This is a mini-submarine used by U.S. Navy **SEAL**s for missions launched from the submarine.

TRIDENT II

The UGM-133 Trident II is a submarine-launched ballistic missile (SLBM) that can carry nuclear warheads, including the W-76 warhead and the W-88 MIRV—multiple independently targeted reentry vehicle.

- The missile is 44 feet long and, like a rocket, it has three stages. The first stage has three rocket motors to lift the Trident into space; the second and third stages each have a single rocket motor to steer the missile over the Earth to the target.

- These rockets give the Trident II a range of 7,000 miles.

- Once near its target, the missile's nose splits open, releasing its warheads. MIRVs can attack separate targets hundreds of miles apart. Each MIRV has a 100-kiloton warhead, with a blast power equal to 1,000 tons of high explosive.

CREW: 155
LENGTH: 560 ft:
SPEED: 14 mph (surface)
23 mph (underwater)
DEPTH: tested down to 800 ft. +

Conning tower, with periscope and communications aerials.

Modern submarines use an advanced sonar system to navigate and to locate targets. Sonar emits and picks up sound waves in order to locate enemy ships and subs. Radar is used on the surface, but sonar is the eyes and ears of the submarine when it is submerged.

All Ohio-class submarines have four torpedo tubes that launch Mk-48 torpedoes with a 640 pound warhead, used to destroy other subs or ships.

Intercontinental Ballistic Missiles

If there is such a thing as the "ultimate weapon," it is the ICBM—intercontinental ballistic missile. ICBMs are fired from underground silos and use technology developed for space flight to hit targets on the other side of the planet. They carry nuclear warheads that can destroy an entire city in one colossal explosion.

THE MINUTEMAN III ICBM

The LGM-130 Minuteman III is the ICBM that makes up the land-based part of America's "nuclear triad"—the other two parts being aircraft armed with nuclear bombs or missiles, and submarines equipped with ballistic missiles. The U.S. has 450 Minuteman ICBMs housed in bombproof underground **silos**, each manned by two officers who can only launch the weapons if the order is confirmed by the president of the United States.

LENGTH: 60 ft.
WEIGHT: 78,000 lb.
SPEED: 15,000 mph (Mach 23—23 times the speed of sound!)
FLIGHT ALTITUDE: 700 mi.
RANGE: 8,000+ mi.

NUCLEAR BLAST POWER

The two nuclear bombs that destroyed the Japanese cities of Hiroshima and Nagasaki at the end of World War II in 1945 had an explosive power of about 15 kilotons. A kiloton blast has roughly the same power as 1,000 tons of high explosive being detonated. The most powerful nuclear weapon ever developed is thought to be America's B-41 nuclear warhead, carried by U.S. Strategic Air Command bombers in the 1960s. It had a warhead rated at 25 megatons.

HOW AN ICBM WORKS

The Minuteman ICBM has three separate rocket stages that take it from launch and into a low orbit around the Earth, before the MIRVs (multiple independently-targeted reentry vehicles) reenter the Earth's atmosphere to strike their targets.

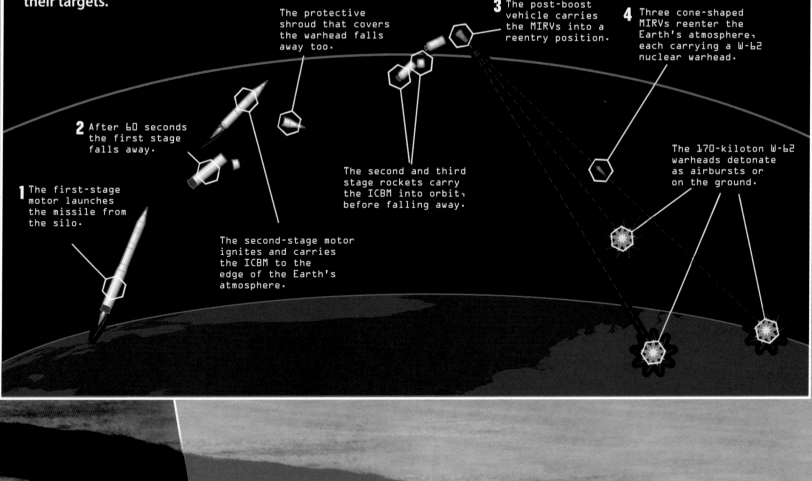

3 The post-boost vehicle carries the MIRVs into a reentry position.

4 Three cone-shaped MIRVs reenter the Earth's atmosphere, each carrying a W-62 nuclear warhead.

The protective shroud that covers the warhead falls away too.

2 After 60 seconds the first stage falls away.

The 170-kiloton W-62 warheads detonate as airbursts or on the ground.

1 The first-stage motor launches the missile from the silo.

The second and third stage rockets carry the ICBM into orbit, before falling away.

The second-stage motor ignites and carries the ICBM to the edge of the Earth's atmosphere.

Glossary

AAM: air to air missile.

AMPHIBIOUS: an amphibious vehicle is one that can operate on both land and water.

APC: armored personnel carrier.

CARBINE: a shorter, lighter version of a standard rifle e.g., the M-4 carbine is a shorter version of the M-16 rifle.

CATERPILLAR TRACKS: a linked band of treads (usually made with plates of metal or rubber) that is turned by two or more wheels. All tanks and many APCs use tracks to help them move over rough ground.

COLD WAR: the name for the period of military and political tension between America and its allies and the Soviet Union (Russia and its allies) that lasted from 1947 to 1989.

COMPOSITE: a man-made material built from a combination of several different substances, such as plastics and metals.

GLOBAL POSITIONING SYSTEM (GPS): a system that uses four or more satellites in space to provide a highly accurate ground location in any weather conditions, day or night.

HACKER: a programmer who illegally or secretly breaks into computer networks.

IED: improvised explosive device.

INFRARED: a type of light that is invisible to the naked eye, but which can be detected as heat. Instruments sensitive to infrared are used by military forces at night and infrared sensors are used by heat-seeking weapons.

LASER: a device that fires a concentrated beam of light. Some laser beams have enough energy to cut through metal.

MACH: the measurement unit for the speed of sound, usually 761.2 mph (Mach 1).

MINE: a hidden or buried explosive device that is automatically detonated by a vehicle or a person coming into contact with it.

PUSHER: a type of propeller mounted at the back of an aircraft, which pushes the airplane forward (most propellers are front-facing "pullers," doing exactly the opposite).

RECONNAISSANCE: gathering information about unknown areas and the strength and positions of enemy forces.

SAM: surface to air missile.

SEAL: name for the U.S. Navy's elite special forces team. "SEAL" stands for "SEa/Air/Land."

SHRAPNEL: metal fragments scattered by an exploding bomb or shell.

SILO: storage and launch facility for nuclear missiles; usually underground as well as heavily fortified and protected against attack.

SMOOTHBORE: a gun barrel that has no rifling—grooves that run the length of the barrel in a spiral pattern, which make the projectile spin. Rifling improves accuracy in most weapons, but modern smoothbore guns usually fire projectiles at such high speed that rifling is not necessary.

SSN/SSBN/SSGN: describe types of submarine. SSN stands for "ship submersible nuclear", B for "ballistic missile" and G for "guided missile."

SUBMUNITION: "munitions" is another name for bombs or shells. Submunitions are smaller weapons (sometimes called bomblets) usually carried in large numbers inside a larger bomb or missile.

SYNTHETIC: a man-made material, such as plastic.

THERMAL: a thermal device, such as a thermal gunsight, uses heat rather than light to detect things (see also Infrared). Thermal sights and sensors work in darkness and low-visibility and are amongst the most advanced target detection systems on a battlefield.

TURBOFAN: a type of engine that uses a fan to push air backward to propel the vehicle forward.

UAV: an unmanned aerial vehicle—either a remote-controlled or robotic flying drone.

Index

The publishers would like to thank the following sources for their kind permission to reproduce the pictures in this book.

Key: t = top, b = bottom, l = left, r = right & c = centre

Copyright © 2013 AeroVironment, Inc: 13cr, 13br

Alamy Images: AlamyCelebrity: 31br

BAE Systems: 9br

Copyright © Boeing: 19tr

Corbis: Aero Graphics, Inc.: 21c; /Thaier Al-Sudani/Reuters: 8-9; /CNP/Sygma: 20t, 21r; /Ed Darack/Science Faction: 5l, 8, 23tr; /Mark Farmer/Transtock: 28bc, 29bc; /Chad Hunt: 4 (meal); /Terry Moore/Stocktrek Images: 36bc; /Dong-Min Jang/ZUMA Press: 34bl, 35cr; /Reuters: 27tr; / Carsten Rehder/dpa: 32bc; /Roger Ressmeyer: 45tr; /Sygma 44; /Peter Turnley: 18-19; /U.S. Navy/Science Faction: 7cr, 10-11; /Philip Wallick: 22-23; /Timm Ziegenthaler/Stocktrek Images: 37tr

DARPA: 11br

U.S. Department of Defense: 3t, 5br, 6-7, 7l, 9cr, 10, 12b, 13tr, 24-25. 25cr, 26-27t, 27cr, 32-33, 33br, 34-35, 35br, 36-37, 37cr, 37br

Getty Images: Alxpin: 30-31; /AFP: 2, 3br, 12; / HIGH-G Productions/Stocktrek Images: 31tr; /Randy Jolly/Timepix/Time Life Pictures: 14-15; /Benjamin Lowy/Edit: 5bc; /Scott Nelson: 16-17; /Joe Raedle: 7br; /Erik Simonsen: 28-29; /Time Life Pictures/DoD: 25tr; /Quavondo: 4, 46-47 (badge)

Lockheed Martin: 23cr, 23br

Courtesy of Northropgrumman.com: 26bc

Courtesy of PEO Soldier: 5cr

© Guy Swarbrick: 38-39

U.S. Air Force: 20-21; /Tech. Sgt. Ken Bergmann 17tr; /Staff Sgt. Dennis J. Henry Jr: 16bc

U.S. Navy: 40l, 40-41, 41r, 42-43, 43r

Every effort has been made to acknowledge correctly and contact the source and/or copyright holder of each picture and Carlton Books Limited apologises for any unintentional errors or omissions, which will be corrected in future editions of this book.

This edition published by Scholastic Inc., 557 Broadway, New York, NY 10012, by arrangement with Carlton Books.

Scholastic and associated logos are trademarks or registered trademarks of Scholastic Inc.

Text, design and illustration © Carlton Books Limited 2013.

10 9 8 7 6 5 4 3 2 1
ISBN: 978-0-545-57093-0
Printed in Dongguan, China.

Senior Editor: Paul Virr
Senior Art Editor: Jake da'Costa
Military Consultant: Captain Dale Dye, Warriors Inc.
Design: Luke Wijsveld
Cover Design: Jake da'Costa
Illustrations: Mark Walker
Picture Research: Ben White
Production: Ena Metagic